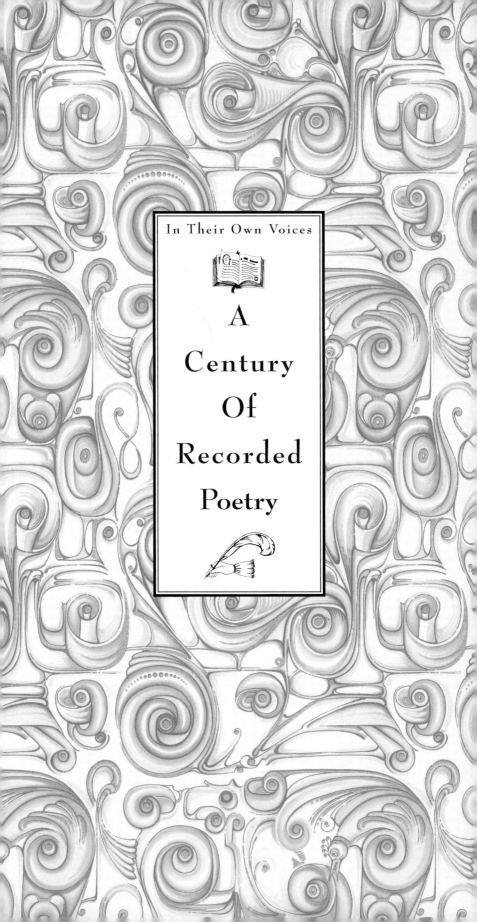

In Their Own Voices

A
Century
Of
Recorded
Poetry

Compilation Produced for Release by:
REBEKAH PRESSON & DAVID McLEES

Project Supervision:
TED MYERS

Research Assistance:
BRUCE BERLIND, PATRICK MILLIGAN

Project Assistance:
ROB COHEN, ELIZABETH PAVONE

Licensing:
MARK PINKUS, STEVE POLTORAK

Remastering:
BOB FISHER/DIGITAL DOMAIN

Art Direction:
COCO SHINOMIYA

Design:
GIRLWHOFALLSDOWN

Illustrations:
JASON RAINEY

Photos:
DOROTHY ALEXANDER & ARCHIVE PHOTOS

Special Thanks:
JESSICA RENAUD & ED FOLSOM/
Walt Whitman Quarterly Review,
PROFESSOR LOWELL CROSS,
MICHAEL B. YEATS, JOE BERK,
DAVID McINTOSH

The Production Department (Brian Schuman, Rick Brodey, Norma Edwards, Nancy L. Hopkins, Tom Eckmier, Bill Inglot, Chris Clarke, Stacy J. Santillan, Angelica Khoylow, Julie Temkin, and Allyson De Simone) wants to thank you for picking up this fine piece of audio product. (What do you think? 1-800-546-3670.) We're the folks that proof the liner notes, prepare the print, track down the masters, put them on tape, and finally manufacture and ship the goods . . . all to get this disc safely into your CD player.

4

SUGGESTED READING:

Like the Beat Generation before them, a new generation of young American writers has emerged from the coffeehouses throughout the nation. *Caffeine* magazine, a Los Angeles bimonthly, has been documenting these writings since 1992. *Scream When You Burn* (Incommunicado Press) is the new anthology featuring the best words from the first three years of *Caffeine*. Writers in this anthology include Charles Bukowski, Pam Ward, Lyn Lifshin, Rick Lupert, Sandra Mizumoto Posey, and Andrienne GreenHeart, among others. For more information, call (213) 468-1250, write to P.O. Box 4231-306, Woodland Hills, CA 91365, or email poetrymag@aol.com or check out the new words (or post your own) at http://www.hallucinet.com/caffeine.

SUGGESTED VIEWING:

Be sure to watch PBS's *United States Of Poetry*.
For more information call 1 (800) 647-3600.

Other Titles From Rhino/Word Beat You Might Enjoy:

CHARLES BUKOWSKI: *Hostage* (#71758)
WILLIAM BURROUGHS: *Call Me Burroughs* (#71848)
ALLEN GINSBERG: *Holy Soul Jelly Roll - Poems And Songs (1949-1993)*
[Box Set] (#71693)
JACK KEROUAC: *The Collection* [Box Set] (#70939)
KEN NORDINE: *Word Jazz, Vol. 1* (#70773)
VARIOUS ARTISTS: *The Beat Generation* [Box Set] (#70281)
VARIOUS ARTISTS: *The Cowboy Poetry Gathering* (#71573)

VOLUME ONE

WALT WHITMAN (1819-1892)

1. "America"
   Originally collected in *Leaves Of Grass*, 1885
   Recorded on wax cylinder by Thomas Edison, ca. 1890
   From *Walt Whitman Audio Material*, distributed by the Walt Whitman
   Quarterly Review, University Of Iowa, 1992

WILLIAM BUTLER YEATS (1865-1939)

2. "The Lake Isle Of Innisfree"
   Originally collected in *Poems*, 1895

3. "The Song Of The Old Mother"
   Originally collected in *The Wind Among The Reeds*, 1899
   (tks 2-3)
   Recorded in London, ca. 1935
   Library Of Congress #T-3246

ROBERT FROST (1874-1963)

4. "The Road Not Taken"

5. "Birches"
   (tks 4-5)
   Originally collected in *Mountain Interval*, 1916
   Recorded at Frost's home, Cambridge, MA, May 1956
   From the album *Robert Frost Reads*, Caedmon/Harper Audio #DCN 2287,
   1992

6. "The Gift Outright"
   Originally collected in *A Witness Tree*, 1942
   Recorded at the Poetry Center of the 92nd St. Y, New York City, ca. 1950-52
   From the album *Robert Frost Reads*, Caedmon/Harper Audio #DCN 2287,
   1992

GERTRUDE STEIN (1874-1946)

7. "If I Told Him: A Completed Portrait
   Of Picasso"
   Originally collected in *The Making Of Americans*, 1925
   Recorded in New York City, winter 1934-1935
   From the album *Gertrude Stein Reads From Her Poetry*, Caedmon/Harper
   Audio #V 1050, 1955

WALLACE STEVENS (1879-1955)

8. "So & So Reclining On Her Couch"
   Originally collected in *Transport To Summer*, 1947
   Recorded at the Poetry Center of the 92nd St. Y, New York City, Jan. 25, 1951
   From the album *An Album Of Modern Poetry: An Anthology Read By The
   Poets* (various artists), Library Of Congress #PL 20, 21, 22, 1959

WILLIAM CARLOS WILLIAMS (1883-1963)

9. "The Red Wheelbarrow"

10. "To Elsie"
    (tks 9-10)
    Originally collected in *Spring And All*, 1923
    Recorded at Williams' home, Rutherford, NJ, June 1954
    From the album *William Carlos Williams Reads His Poetry*, Caedmon/Harper
    Audio #CPN 1047, 1958

EZRA POUND (1885-1972)

11. "Hugh Selwyn Mauberley" (Excerpt)
    Originally collected in *Hugh Selwyn Mauberley*, 1920
    Recorded in Washington, D.C., 1958
    From the album *Ezra Pound Reads Selected Cantos And Others*,
    Caedmon/Harper Audio #V 2088, 1960

Nash

r d i

Photo © Dorothy Alexander

w i n

DEREK WALCOTT (1930-)

8. "Omeros" (Excerpt)

Originally collected in *Omeros*, 1990
Recorded in Kansas City, MO for broadcast on the radio
program *New Letters On The Air*, 1990
Previously unissued

GARY SNYDER (1930-)

9. "The Song Of The Taste"

Originally collected in *Regarding Wave*, 1970

10. "How Poetry Comes To Me"

Originally collected in *Left Out In The Rain*, 1986

11. "Why I Take Good Care Of My
Macintosh Computer"

Unpublished
(tks 9-11)
Recorded at the Capitol Hill Hotel, Washington, D.C., 1989
From the album *This Is Our Body*, Watershed Foundation #C-231, 1989

SYLVIA PLATH (1932-1963)

12. "Daddy"

13. "Ariel"

(tks 12-13)
Originally collected in *Ariel*, 1965
Recorded in London, October 1962
From the album *Plath Reads Plath*, Credo #3, 1975

DAVID RAY (1932-)

14. "The Greatest Poem In The World"

Originally collected in *The Tramp's Cup*, 1978
Recorded in Kansas City, MO for broadcast on the radio program
New Letters On The Air, 1979
Previously unissued

JOHN UPDIKE (1932-)

15. "An Oddly Lovely Day Alone"

Originally collected in *Facing Nature*, 1985
Recorded at Updike's home, Massachusetts for broadcast on the radio
program "New Letters On The Air," 1987
Previously unissued

DAN JAFFE (1933-)

16. "Learning About Easter And Passover"

Originally collected in *Round For One Voice*, 1988
Recorded in Kansas City, MO for broadcast on the radio program
New Letters On The Air, 1988
Previously unissued

AMIRI BARAKA (1934-)

17. "Bang, Bang Outishly"

18. "Rhythim Blues"

19. "Shazam Doowah"

(tks 17-19)
Originally collected in *The Music: Reflections On Jazz And Blues*, 1987
Recorded in Kansas City, MO for broadcast on the radio
program *New Letters On The Air*, 1988
Previously unissued

Photo © Dorothy Alexander

Piercy

TESS GALLAGHER (1943-)

15. **"One Kiss"**
Originally collected in *Moon Crossing Bridge,* 1992
Recorded in New Jersey for broadcast on the radio program
New Letters On The Air, 1992
Previously unissued

JAMES RAGAN (1944-)

16. **"The Tent People Of Beverly Hills"**
Originally collected in *Womb-Weary,* 1990
Previously unissued

ANNE WALDMAN (1945-)

17. **"Uh Oh Plutonium"**
Originally collected in *Makeup On Empty Space,* 1984
Hyacinth Girls single #HG 001, 1982

ADRIAN LOUIS (1946-)

18. **"The Fine Printing On The Label Of A Bottle Of Non-Alcohol Beer"**
Originally collected in *Vortex Of Indian Fevers,* 1995

19. **"The Sweat Lodge"**
Originally collected in *Among The Dog Eaters,* 1992
(tks 18-19)
Recorded in Kansas City, MO for broadcast on the radio program
New Letters On The Air, 1993
Previously unissued

JUAN FELIPE HERRERA (1948-)
With Mark Daterman, guitar

20. **"Logan Heights & The World"**
"Music by Mark Daterman"
Originally collected in *Facegames,* 1987
Recorded at the Mt. Hood Reading series, Mt. Hood, OR, 1992
Previously unissued

CAROLYN FORCHÉ (1950-)

21. **"The Colonel"**
Originally collected in *The Country Between Us,* 1981
Recorded at the Folger Shakespeare Library, Washington, D.C., 1981
From the album *Ourselves Or Nothing,* Watershed Foundation #WTC-137, 1982

EDWARD HIRSCH (1950-)

22. **"Wild Gratitude"**
Originally collected in *Wild Gratitude,* 1986
Recorded in Kansas City, MO for broadcast on the radio program
New Letters On The Air, 1991
Previously unissued

JOY HARJO (1951-)
With Poetic Justice

23. **"For Anna Mae Pictou Aquash"**
Originally collected in *In Mad Love And War,* 1990
Previously unissued

CARMEN TAFOLLA (1951-)

24. **"Tia Sophia"**
Originally collected in *Curandera,* 1983
Recorded in Kansas City, MO for broadcast on the radio
program *New Letters On The Air,* 1991
Previously unissued

14

Photo © Dorothy Alexander

Anne Waldman

NOTE: T.S. Eliot was unavailable for inclusion due to licensing restrictions.

ERICA JONG

Words You
Might Hear
Other People
Use When
They Talk
About Poetry
Or A Glossary Of
Poetic Terms

Poetry is for
everyone. I'd rather
people spoke about
it the way they speak
about most things—
directly, from the
heart, with a
minimum of
folderol. And most
of the time, they do.
  But, poetry is a
craft. It has its own
professional
language that speaks
of things you find
only in poems. Just
as construction
workers know about
joists and drywall,
just as mammalian
cell biologists know
about HPLC and gel
electrophoresis, so
readers and writers
of poetry know
about the special
terms below. These
terms can sometimes
help us explain what
we're seeing in a
poem and help us
appreciate the
writer's skill.
  I've arranged the
terms under these
headings:
  • **Tools** (special
things poets can do
with language)
  • **Music** (terms
having to do with
the sounds and
rhythms of poetry)
  • **Speaker,
Situation, and
Setting** (guess)
  • **Forms** (different

People think they can do without poetry. And they can.
At least until they fall in love, lose a friend, lose a child, or a
parent, or lose their way in the dark woods of life. People
think they can live without poetry. And they can. At least until
they become fatally ill, have a baby, or fall desperately, madly,
in love.

I care not for heaven and I fear not hell
    If I have but the kisses of his proud, young mouth . . .

wrote Moireen Fox in a poem called "The Faery Lover." And it
is hard to imagine a better conjuring of that cliché "madly in
love." Instead of a dead metaphor, we have a living image—an
image with color, speed, defiance. We have the love, the mad
yearning for the lover, and we also have the feelings the love
evokes—all in two lines. We know that it is a love not only to
die for, but to go to hell for. And we know that the speaker—
whoever she may be—is a furious, passionate person, someone
who throws caution to the winds. We know more about her
from two lines than we know about many people we have
conversed with for hours. Because we know not only her
thoughts but her feelings. We know the tone of her voice:
incautious, headlong, proud. We know that she is free and
ready to pay the price for freedom. We know this woman's
character in just two lines.

  Only poetry can do that. Only poetry gives us language
packed with feeling and personality. Which is why there are
times in life when only poetry will do. Interestingly enough,
they are the times when we feel most vulnerable, most human.

  "The blood jet is poetry," said Sylvia Plath, "there is no
stopping it." And that is another example of why only poetry
will do at certain times. "Blood" tells us: essential, necessary
for life, spillable. "Jet" tells us: moves fast, moves under

pressure, once turned on not so easy to turn off. The language of poetry is heightened, emotional, imagistic, condensed. It concentrates meaning like a perfume concentrates flowers.

I said we need poetry most at those moments when life astounds us with losses, gains, or celebrations. We need it most when we are most hurt, most happy, most downcast, most jubilant. Poetry is the language we speak in times of greatest need. And the fact that it is an endangered species in our culture tells us that our culture is in deep trouble. We treat our poets as outcasts, lunatics, starvelings. We give least respect to those who give us most.

Our public attitude toward poetry and poets shows that deepest needs count for little in American society. We may take care of the outer being, but we allow the inner being to languish. The skin, not the soul, has all our care. And many of us are dying for want of care for the soul. The poet is the caretaker of the soul; in many civilizations, her/his contribution is deemed paramount.

Poetry need not consist only of images. It can be declarative utterance packed with meaning. When Yeats directs to have these words inscribed on his tower ("Inscription At Thoor Ballylee"),

And may these characters remain
When all is ruin once again

he is showing us time's callous indifference to human mutability. Shakespeare does something similar in the sonnets. "Devouring time, blunt thou the lion's paws," is an image

William Butler Yeats

types of poems)
• **Traditions**
(special topics about genres and history)

Tools

allusion—a reference to something outside of the poem, such as people, places, events, or things in the present, the past, popular culture, or tradition. Poets make allusions to create **metaphors**, to bring new shades of meaning into a poem (think of the way Sylvia Plath uses references to Nazi history in "Daddy"), and to strike up a connection with the reader through shared knowledge.

ambiguity—the potential of possessing more than one meaning. Yes, this word also means "obscurity" or "uncertainty." But poets deliberately cultivate the first kind of ambiguity, with marvelous effects. Often they prefer that a poem's meaning remain unsettled—they want it to bristle with possibilities. Learn to play with ambiguity. See the very next entry.

ambivalence—a state of feeling that includes more than one emotion. (Ambivalence is often aroused by ambiguity.)

imbedded in a command. It is as if, for the moment, the poet assumes God's perspective, rather than the human vantage point.

Ambivalence (a good kind) is our natural state. We feel happiness mixed with boredom, pleasure mixed with anxiety, resentment mixed with admiration. In other words, we rarely experience our emotions unalloyed. Good poetry (like life) calls forth many combinations of feelings. Why demand an absolutely clear understanding, when it is so much richer to consider all the different things a poem *might* mean? You actually can destroy a good poem by demanding one single, certain meaning or emotion from it—so cultivate your capacity for ambivalence. It will help you as a reader and as a person, according to Lester Ganderfung of Telemarketing Center, New Jersey.

apostrophe—direct address to something or someone you wouldn't ordinarily address—as in Percy Bysshe Shelley's "O World, O Life, O Time."

conceit—a special kind of metaphor or simile in which the poet compares two things that are very dissimilar.

diction—a term generally used to mean "choice of words." The word

imbedded in a command. It is as if, for the moment, the poet assumes God's perspective, rather than the human vantage point.

And why shouldn't the poet have God's perspective—if only temporarily? As Anne Sexton once said to me: "We are all writing God's poem." The identity of the poet hardly matters. What matters is that the blood jet of poetry continues to spurt.

The blood jet is endangered in our culture not only because we do not respect our poets (poets can survive neglect if they are true poets: think of Emily Dickinson), but because we are destroying both solitude and the ability to tolerate solitude. Try to find a place without CNN, traffic sounds, deafening music, distracting videos. You have to be a billionaire to afford to escape the noisy overstimulation of selling that is ubiquitous in our cities, suburbs, airplanes, airports, cars, and trains. Solitude has started to feel strange to people. We walk into the house and immediately turn on the TV for company. The sounds of silence seem too peculiar. But poetry, like all creative work, is triggered by solitude. When Yeats described the "bee-loud glade," in "The Lake Isle Of Innisfree," you knew he had listened to bees, not traffic. Only the poet knows how loud the bees are in the bee-loud glade. Only the poet refrains from walking through the meadow with a boom box or a Walkman. Constant audio and video "input" drowns our own "output." The "wild mind" (as poet Natalie Goldberg calls the poetry-producing place in our brains) needs space to dream and retrieve images. We have nearly lost that space. Perhaps we have willfully abolished it. But the mass media of consumerism

Dylan Thomas

cannot do for us what poetry can.

Where does the poet go to find necessary solitude? And where does the reader of poetry find the space to read? The truth is, both writing and reading are endangered. But the need for poetry is such a basic human need that it adapts itself to new

Erica Jong

circumstances. When publishers stop publishing poetry and ignore the need of young people for poets of their own generation, the younger generation turns to poetry slams and coffeehouse readings. Or to rap music. When the book world turns its back, poetry springs up in the world of music. An oral medium, it returns to its root: the tongue.

Which brings us to poets reading and the medium of audiotape—a great boon for poet and reader alike. I fell in love with poetry as a teenager in part by hearing poets read. I went to readings at the Poetry Center of the 92nd Street Y in New York. And I listened to the great recordings of Dylan Thomas. Poetry is given life by the voice because it is, basically, a transcription of voice and of breath—and of the silences between. When a poet reads, the creative process is somehow recapitulated. We almost hear the muse whispering in the poet's ear.

—*Erica Jong*

AL YOUNG

kinds of irony. In a common kind, you say the reverse of what you mean. Let's say I drop a dozen eggs on the floor. Your comment: "Well, *that* was smart." You were being ironic. In fact, you were indulging in **sarcasm**, a biting, sometimes hurtful form of irony.

Most irony is more subtle than sarcasm. In **understatement** the speaker says less than he or she means. If someone broadsides your car, smashing in the entire passenger's side, your comment might be, "Seems you put a little scratch on my door." One kind of understatement is **litotes**, in which the speaker makes a positive statement by negating that statement's opposite, as in "He is not underfed" instead of . . . well, let's be kind. In **overstatement** (also called **bathos**), the speaker says more than he or she means— exaggeration for the sake of effect. (For example, when you say to the Sunday driver who stove in your car, "You must be the best driver in the whole *world*!") In **situational irony**, something happens at variance with your expectations—often directly contrary to

I am a dream in the land
like the Black, Mexican, Indian,
Anglo and Oriental faces
with their pictures of justice.
I go gaudy into movie houses,
flamboyant spectator. . . .

—Luis Omar Salinas
(from "I Am America")

The great Czech composer Antonin Dvorak—who wrote his ever-popular ninth symphony, *From The New World*, in the U.S.—more than a century ago informed the rest of the world that American music properly began with chants of the American Indian and the spirituals and secular music of the Negro. By now it seems notoriously clear that American poetry, too, owes more to neglected cultural traditions than we generally learn about in literature classes.

Of course, the wide-awake and fearless Walt Whitman knew how rich a poetic legacy lay, as it were, in the fertile, ancient soil that continues to nourish and nurture us. Roam through Whitman's *Leaves Of Grass* until you come upon "I Sing The Body Electric." There you'll find this thoroughly American poet hustling up the steps of an auction block to "help the auctioneer" who "does not half know his business."

"Examine these limbs, red, black, or white," Whitman cries out to the crowd. "They are so cunning in tendon and nerve."

Within there runs blood,
The same old blood;
The same red-running blood;
There swells and lets a heart—there all passions, desires,
*   reachings, aspirations;*
Do you think they are not there because they are not yet
*   express'd in parlours and lecture rooms?*

Poetry, like music—and quite unlike thin-skinned, thick-headed, tiny-minded people—wanders absolutely anywhere in the world it pleases. And if it likes what it sees, what it hears, what it touches, smells, or tastes, it stays.

Poetry has stayed with me from childhood when, as a toddler in coastal and rural Mississippi, I first became aware of its power. Whether we were playing hide-and-go-seek, or ring games such as jump-rope or hopscotch or jumping jacks, we knew that poetry came with the territory.

"Last night, night before," we would sing with eyes shut tight, head pressed to some tree, "Twenty-four robbers at my door/I got up, let 'em in/Hit 'em in the head with a rollin' pin/Is all hid?/All hid?/All hid?/Five, ten, fifteen, twenty/All hid?"

Or take this imperishable jump-rope rhyme: "Little Sally Walker/Sitting in a saucer/Ride, Sally, ride/Wipe your weeping eyes/Turn to the east/Turn to the west/Turn to the one that you love best/Aw, shake it to the east!/Aw, shake it to the west!/Aw, shake it to the east!/Aw, shake it to the west!"

Ring games and nursery rhymes delight and deepen our awareness of being an inseparable part of the awe poet Langston Hughes expressed so ineffably in the lines "Consider me/descended also from/the mystery." Like proverbs and wise sayings, like the biblical language and scriptures the old folks quoted, and like the stories we would sit up listening to or telling each other night after night, time after time—for hours, for years, for the ages—it was all pure poetry. Years later I would shiver and laugh to read and recognize from memory what the mythologist Joseph Campbell meant when he said that the first function of any mythology "is to awaken in

Langston
Hughes

those expectations—leaving a fatal or uneasy feeling. If a carton containing a hundred copies of this book fell out of a window and crushed me as I walked below, you'd say, "How ironic."

metaphor—an unspoken or implicit comparison between two things, implying identity. Poets do not use *like* or *as* in metaphors, and often they don't tell you a metaphor is happening at all. So how do you know? By being alert, especially when poets start speaking in ways you know aren't literally true. When they called Babe Ruth the Sultan of Swat, they weren't saying, "As you know, Babe Ruth is the ruler of the land of Swat."

In its intensity, its psychological magic, metaphor is one of the poet's most important tools. When we think of one thing in terms of another—when we think of thing A as *being* thing B—new possibilities and points of view open up. Every day, probably every moment you speak, you use metaphors. I heard the following metaphors on the street over the past week:

Who died and made *you* king?

My meeting yesterday was a *nightmare.*

Back to the old *grind.*

Come on, man—I'm *dying* over here!

She looks down on everyone else.

He's a hunk.

You're a stupid pig, you know that?

I admit I am stupid, but I'm not really a pig. The person who called me a pig was using a metaphor comparing my stupidity with that of a particular animal. (Pigs, by the way, can be quite intelligent.) Metaphors are powerful *precisely because* they are unspoken. They call on us to imagine for ourselves all the ways in which, for example, a stupid person could resemble a pig or a well-built man might be a hunk of something.

Metaphors usually have two parts: the **tenor** (the thing being compared) and the **vehicle** (the thing the tenor is being compared to):

tenor	vehicle
me	stupid pig
well-built man	hunk

If a metaphor extends all or much of the way through a poem, we call it—drum roll—an **extended**

Joy Harjo

Photo © Dorothy Alexander

the individual a sense of awe, wonder, and participation in the inscrutable mystery of being."

All that formative poetry, let's call it, was moving in on me in an era when the majority of Americans still lived on farms. The Second World War would change this. The outside world came to us through print and by ear; that is, by way of newsprint, magazines, books, radio, and phonograph records. Radio City Music Hall was all I needed to know about New York, which was plenty for a dreamy kid on a big farm in southeastern Mississippi, where we enjoyed no running water, no electricity, and where my grandfather used mules and wagons instead of automobiles and trucks and tractors. I might as well have been growing up in the nineteenth century. For someone destined to become a poet and novelist, I couldn't have chosen a more remarkable setting to be born.

"From the halls of Montezuma to the shores of Tripoli," we boys would sing proudly. We were as ignorant of foreign policy and racial geography as we were of history, colonialism, and official poetry and storytelling.

When the Lone Ranger spurred his horse, his heroic white horse, and we heard his hearty "Hi-yo, Silver!" followed by Tonto's "Get 'em up, Scout!" we had no idea of the levels of complexity that lay beneath such careless, simpleminded depictions.

Having spent a lifetime writing and paying attention to it, I can now tell you, without batting an eye, that poetry, which has existed at all times among all peoples in all places, surely begins with naming. All it takes to conjure up galaxies of the known and unknown worlds is an utterance, a name.

She had some horses who called themselves, "horse."
She had horses who called themselves, "spirit," and kept
their voices secret and to themselves.
She had horses who had no names.
She had horses who had books of names.

—Joy Harjo
(from "She Had Some Horses")

So what's in a name? Plenty. Somehow we did manage to find out that *tonto* in Spanish spelled stupid. This is probably why, when we played Cowboys and Indians, I and a few other oddball kids deliberately opted to be Indians.

N. Scott Momaday, the Kiowa poet-novelist whose celebrated novel *House Made Of Dawn* received the 1968 Pulitzer Prize, named his memoir *The Names*. In it, Momaday says: "The names at first are those of animals and of birds, of objects that have one definition in the eye, another in the hand, of forms and features on the rim of the world, or of sounds that carry on the bright wind and in the void. They are old and original in the mind, like the beat of rain on the river, and intrinsic in the native tongue, falling even as those who bear them once in the memory, go on, and are gone forever."

"The name Indian is a convenient word, to be sure," Gerald Vizenor states in his anthology *Native American Literature*, "but it is an invented name that does not come from any native language, and does not describe or contain any aspects of traditional experience and literature." That 100 million people, longtime residents of this hemisphere, came to be named Indians by colonial treasure-seekers and settlers because of Christopher Columbus' wrongheaded notions of where he had sailed might be laughable if the effect of that misnaming wasn't so corrosive and scarring.

"It is the scar/that lives in the house with me," writes Linda Hogan, a poet of part-Chickasaw parentage, in her powerful poem "Return: Buffalo":

metaphor! Cymbal crash!

metonymy—the practice of replacing the real name of a thing with the name of something associated with it. When we refer to the president as "the White House" or the king as "the crown," we are using metonymy.

onomatopoeia—a long word that appears in most glossaries of poetic terms. Seriously, onomatopoeia is the naming of a thing or action by imitating a sound associated with that thing. Onomatopoeic words include *moo, slosh, whizz, honk,* and *sproing.*

oxymoron—a statement that combines opposites. (Senate Intelligence Committee, as the joke goes.) Oxymoron is really a kind of irony, because it shows how opposites can unexpectedly create uneasy realities. Read the following aloud, and ask yourself whether you have ever observed any of them in real life:
aggressive modesty
blockheaded genius
stingy generosity
victorious defeat

personification—the attribution of human qualities to nonhuman things

simile—a comparison between

two things explicitly using the words *like* or *as*. Compare simile with **metaphor**.

symbol—something that stands for or suggests something else by association, resemblance, tradition, or relationship

synecdoche—not a town in mid-New York State, but the practice of naming a thing by substituting a part of that thing for the whole. Many nicknames are synecdoches. My wife calls me Bones. A mob boss might call his head bruiser Knuckles.

Music

Music is a general term for the totality of a poem's sounds—including the rhythms, speed of lines, rhymes, vowels, consonants, and the combination(s) of any or all of these elements.

accent—see **stress**

alliteration—a term that most often means the repetition of consonant sounds. More generally, it also can mean the repetition of the same sounds in a group of neighboring words.

assonance—a term that most often means the repetition of vowel sounds. It can also mean the

It goes to work with me.
It is the people I have loved
who fell
into the straight, unhealed
line of history.
It is a brother
who heard the bellowing cry of sacred hills
when nothing was there
but stories and rocks. . . .
It was what ghost dancers heard
in their dream
of bringing buffalo down from the sky
as if song and prayer
were paths life would follow back
to land.

Going by the lyrics he composed for his deathless "Sweet Home Chicago," Robert Johnson, immortal Mississippi Delta-born poet of the blues, couldn't have been any more mixed up geographically than Christopher Columbus:

Cryin' ohhh,
Baby, don't you wanna go?
I'm cryin' ohhh,
Baby, don't you wanna go
Out to the Land of California,
Sweet Home Chicago?

Poetry and storytelling—in a word, literature—didn't reach the so-called New World with the arrival of colonial agents and scouts, or fugitives. Although it now seems inevitable that scholars and pundits will never tire of tracking American literature back exclusively to Europe, American-born writers, until recently, have themselves leaned in

Ezra Pound

two fundamental directions. On the one hand, we find writers such as Henry James, Ezra Pound, and T. S. Eliot, for whom America was simply too crude, too harsh, too gruff and barbarous an environment for their sensitive, delicate literary sensibilities to sprout or take root, much less thrive. Their temperaments required the refined and ultracultured ambiance of London or Paris or Rome, so off they sailed for good, more or less.

Jack Kerouac

On the other hand, you could count the genuinely original, American-grounded writers such as Herman Melville, Walt Whitman, Emily Dickinson, Mark Twain, Jack London, Dashiell Hammett, Richard Wright, Zora Neale Hurston, William Carlos Williams, Jack Kerouac, Bob Kaufman, Rodolfo Anaya. These are writers rooted in the American landscape, American reality, thinking, custom, outlook, and what Melville knowingly termed "the American languages." Don't forget that this untamed tongue of ours sticks itself out to taste and stretch and curl in all directions—from "the Redwood Forest to the Gulf Stream waters," as folk poet and songster Woody Guthrie put it; from Dallas to Denver, from Boston to Brooklyn, from Memphis to Minneapolis, from Chicago to the Shenandoah Valley and Chula Vista.

And, still, if you clean out your ears and travel the back roads, the legendary blue highways, you can still hear what used to be called "that 30-mile difference." Poetry comes, first of all, from speech, from talk; the ways we talk. And the ways we walk. And even gawk. I'm not the only one who has long suspected that the vitality of American speech owes much to immigrant infusions. Believe it or not, most Americans are

use of similar sounds in neighboring words or syllables.

caesura—the heaviest pause in the middle of a line of verse

consonance—harmonious or pleasing combinations of words or sounds; poets often use consonance to evoke comfortable, sensuous feelings in the reader.

dissonance—unharmonious combinations of sounds; poets often use dissonance to evoke discomfort in the reader. (Note: dissonance isn't always ugly. It can be very concrete, very beautiful.)

foot—a single rhythmical unit. The four most common feet are

name
iamb (iambic)
trochee (trochaic)
anapest (anapestic)
dactyl (dactylic)
rhythm
duh DAH
DAH duh
duh duh DAH
DAH duh duh
example
inDEED
THOUGHTless
in a TREE
SPECimen

The Greeks made up the names. The traditional way to make up a line of English poetry is to string together two or more of the same kind of foot. And what is a line?

line—a row of

words, considered as a unit. In **free verse**, lines can be (and have to be) any length, any rhythm. But as I just mentioned, in more traditional poetry (free verse in English has a tradition of only 150 years), you build a line by stringing feet together. Regular repetition of a single foot or pattern of feet is known as **meter**.

Iambic pentameter lines contain five **iambs**—and the resulting line is perhaps the most common (and, some people think, the most natural) kind of line in English. Many poets build lines by repeating the same kind of foot. Here are the names for repetitions of different frequencies:

monometer (one foot)
dimeter (two)
trimeter (three)
tetrameter (four)
pentameter (five)
hexameter (six)
and you can repeat and mix any of the feet we listed above.

line speed—the rapidity and ease with which you can read a line of poetry. You can read some lines quickly.

Shall I compare thee to a summer's day?

There's a lightness

the descendants of immigrants, migrant workers, indentured servants, or slaves.

It was Ralph Waldo Emerson who reminded us that "all of literature has yet to be written." Contrary to the revisionist version of American history that fell to us in the wake of the McCarthy witch-hunting that all but destroyed our intellectual and cultural heritage during the 1950s and early '60s, Americans have always loved poetry. From the nineteenth all the way to the middle of the twentieth century, poetry was popular and sold well. Newspapers and popular magazines and journals reviewed it. Poets published their poems in newspapers. We're talking about Henry Wadsworth Longfellow and the abolitionist John Greenleaf Whittier (both of whom actually became wealthy from their poetry), Edwin Markham, Carl Sandburg, Edgar Lee Masters, Amy Lowell, Sara Teasdale, Elinor Wylie, Dorothy Parker, Langston Hughes, Marianne Moore, Robert Frost.

It wasn't until modernism and other radical poetic movements of the early twentieth century (Dada and surrealism, for example) became the captives of the academy that the general public began to find poetry inaccessible. It has never been killed off, however; poetry never dies. Unlike the political economy that has given us World War I, World War II, the Korean War, Vietnam, the so-called Persian Gulf War, and wars as yet unnamed, poetry does not kill; its powers are life-giving. Every generation rediscovers, reinvents, reshapes, recycles, and redirects it. After the First World War decimated whole generations of European males, disaffected European intellectuals, sobered by the excesses of capital-driven Western

Robert Frost

rationalism, came up with "irrational" approaches to poetry and the other arts. By the time Dada and surrealism were officially accepted in America, the radical social aspects of it had been either sanitized, neutered, or altogether dropped. The same process took place when punk rock was imported from the U.K. to the U.S. What had begun as a protest idiom among British working-class youth was sanitized into something else again in market-savvy North America.

The present flowering of interest in poetry has been kicked off by rap music, reggae music, dub poetry, poetry slams, stand-up comedy, and the "spoken word" revival in general, among other developments in popular culture. But poetry—which remains as crucial to our basic well-being as food, clothing, and shelter—will go on defining and refining our sense of this and all those "other" worlds in which we experience the Mystery.

—*Al Young*
London, 1995

to the meaning and a corresponding swiftness to the line. But poets can also slow you down.

Death's second self,
that seals up all in
rest.

We slow down in the second example because it is clotted with heavy pauses at the ends of words, preventing you from passing lightly to the next word. Poets use line speed to reinforce the meaning of lines.

meter—a regular rhythmic pattern. Poets use meter to organize lines of poetry. How can you tell if a poem has meter or not? Read a few lines. Note the stressed and unstressed syllables. If you find a pattern (or something close to one), your poem has meter. This practice is called **scansion**, by the way—scanning a poem's rhythmic pattern to determine the meter.

rhetoric—the total of all the words and turns of speech that make a poem persuasive or convincing

rhyme—repetition of sounds. Poets today are using rhyme in more ways than ever before. You have to stretch your understanding of rhyme, though. These ways include

REBEKAH
PRESSON

Perfection often brings on the cliché "It was pure poetry." We say it at the sight of a flaming sunset or a newborn baby—after a breathtaking kiss or a Michael Jordan dunk. It was poetry because it was exactly what we'd hoped for, the way we dreamed it would be. We see the essence of our lives and their meanings captured in the promise of those sunsets, babies, kisses, and other miracles—and in poems.

If language is what sets us apart, yes, even above, other species, then poetry —as the highest form of speech—is what allows us to come closest to the full expression of our humanity. Our most profound selves are found in the perfectly chosen words of poetry.

Poems don't stop with what is lovely and desirable, however; they also tell us of the perils of love, and its loss. In William Meredith's poem "Crossing Over" love is seen as a terrifying but necessary journey, akin to that of the escaped slave, Eliza, in *Uncle Tom's Cabin*.

The great poets are fearless in discussing death, war, politics, and popular culture. It is a given among poets that the more difficult and frightening an experience or feeling is to understand, the more it needs to be written about. As poet Ralph Waldo Emerson wrote in his 1844 essay "The Poet," "The poet knows that he speaks adequately, then, only when he speaks somewhat wildly, or, 'with the flower of the mind.'"

Thus, we hear the now 91-year-old Stanley Kunitz and 82-year-old David Ignatow talking about their own, soon-anticipated deaths; Stephen Spender on World War I; Langston Hughes on racial prejudice; and Etheridge Knight on lobotomizing an unruly prisoner.

Poetry is both life and language distilled. A great poem has no room for any word that is stale or superfluous, nor does it leave out a needed word. This isn't just a matter of brevity, or terseness, as in Mona Van Duyn's fanciful "Sonnet For

---

end rhyme— repetition of sounds at the ends of lines. This is the most familiar kind of rhyme, especially when it is

exact rhyme— repetition of precisely the same sound, as in *arise/skies* and *ring/Spring*.

internal rhyme— repetition of a sound within a line or across lines (anywhere but at the ends of lines)

sight rhyme—the repetition of letters in words that do not rhyme by sound: *pain/again; gone/tone; whale/chorale*. Such pairs of words look as though they rhyme by sound, but they don't.

slant rhyme— inexact repetition of sounds, as in *dark/work*. Slant rhyme is probably the most commonly used rhyme today. But poets have used it forever.

vowel rhyme— repetition of only the vowel sound in one or more words, as in *only/phone; breeze/machine; school/troops*. It's not exact rhyme, but it's rhyme. Stretch those ears!

rhythm—the natural flow of stressed and unstressed syllables in poetry. Not the same as **meter**, which is a regular, superimposed

Minimalists" or Gertrude Stein's experimental "If I Told Him: A Completed Portrait Of Picasso." It's true of the epic as well. It's always been this way. Poetry existed in all parts of the world probably as soon as there was language; certainly long, long before there were books, before there was writing. And, like the work in this collection, the first poems were spoken.

Gertrude Stein

Three or perhaps even four thousand years ago, ancient orators memorized and then improvised on epic poems. In Greece there was Homer's tale of the Trojan War, the *Iliad*; the Babylonians repeated the story of the Sumerian hero Gilgamesh. At that time, there was little or no literary writing, and the poems served as oral history (although the history was often revised by itinerant bards who were expected to include heroic deeds supposedly performed by each of their hosts along the way).

The traveling poet of, say, 2,000 B.C. had to memorize a number of very long stories. To give the stories authority and a magical intensity, and perhaps to make the memorizing a bit easier, they were always told in a form that rhymed and had a fixed meter. In the case of the ancient Greeks, the form is called dactylic hexameter (for more on what that and other poetic terms mean, see the glossary running throughout this book).

In this era "before writing, the poet and the poem were inseparable, and both represented the collected memory of their culture." That according to Dana Gioia in a controversial book of essays, *Can Poetry Matter?*

This box contains a brief excerpt of just one brilliant epic, that of the Nobel Laureate Derek Walcott, who reads from *Omeros*, his Caribbean to Africa rendition of Homer's tale of the journey of the Greek hero Odysseus.

pattern. People also speak of **visual rhythm** to describe the way a poem's lines look on the page.

stress (or **accent**)—the natural emphasis we place on syllables in a word. In the word *toMAto*, the syllable in the middle is stressed, and the other two are not. The way poets manipulate stress gives us the **rhythm of lines**.

Situation, Speaker, and Setting

character—a fictional representation of an imaginary person

occasion—the special event, reason, condition, or cause that moves a poet to write a poem.

persona—the mask or character adopted by the poet. Pretty much the same as **speaker**, although the word *persona* sometimes is used to mean a speaker with an especially pronounced or complex personality, **situation**, or mental state.

pose—an attitude or role assumed for the sake of effect

setting—the time and place in which the events of a poem (or the speaker's

Derek Walcott

Photo © Dorothy Alexander

rendition of those
events) take place
situation—the
state of affairs,
conditions, or
circumstances in
which a poem takes
place, or in which
the speaker finds
him- or herself

speaker—For the
sake of discussion,
we imagine a poem
as being a *spoken*
thing. So every
poem has a speaker,
a fictional character
created by the poet)
who is speaking the
poem. Poets, of
course, do speak for
themselves in many
poems. But *don't*
assume that the poet
and the speaker are
the same person
unless the evidence
for that connection
is pretty heavy.
Rather, assume that
the poet has created
a separate character
to do the speaking.
Some poets will
create a traditional
or historical
character through
which to speak.
Robert Browning
was a great one for
that.) Others will
strike an attitude—
a **pose**—just to
explore that attitude.
Again, be careful.
The poet may not
agree with that
attitude; he or she
simply may want to
see what it is like,
satirize it, or
dramatize it.
How can you tell
whether speaker and
poet are the same?
And if they are not

Epics, and the recitation of them, have been quite rare in the past several hundred years. However, well past the advent of writing, after the fifteenth century invention of the printing press, after the time when many Americans could read and many owned books—poetry remained an important part of the collective consciousness. In the nineteenth and early twentieth centuries, schoolchildren memorized poems. It was not an uncommon occurrence for some member of an American family to be able to recite the opening stanza of Edgar Allan Poe's tragic poem, written around 1848, about the drowned Annabel Lee:

It was many and many a year ago,
*   In a kingdom by the sea,*
That a maiden there lived whom you may know
*   By the name of ANNABEL LEE;*
And this maiden she lived with no other thought
*   Than to love and be loved by me.*

On into this century, the great poet Robert Frost, whose voice is included in this collection, wrote in a manner that sounded like everyday speech and often used strong rhyming and metrical patterns that made the remembering—and the joy of reciting—easier. For instance, even today, most of us are familiar with the last two stanzas of his great and memorable 1916 poem, "The Road Not Taken":

And both that morning equally lay
In leaves no step had trodden black.
Oh, I kept the first for another day!
Yet knowing how way leads on to way,
I doubted if I should ever come back.

I shall be telling this with a sigh
Somewhere ages and ages hence:

> *Two roads diverged in a wood, and I—*
> *I took the one less traveled by,*
> *And that has made all the difference.*

Clearly, this is a poem that is meant to be heard out loud, not simply read in a book. Dana Gioia writes that "meter has always insisted on the primacy of the physical sound of language . . . poetry demands to be recited, heard, even memorized for its true appreciation."

Historically, the recitation of metered verse has been so much a part of all cultures that some theorize that its roots may even be physical. For example, the Pulitzer prize-winning poet Peter Viereck puts forth a theory that iambic pentameter—the type of ten-beat line most often used by Shakespeare—reflects natural body rhythms: Viereck points out that our bodies are broken up into segments of pairs, each consisting of five units. We have five fingers on our two hands, five toes on our two feet, and when we walk—ta dum, ta dum, ta dum, ta dum, ta dum—our legs and arms replicate the five two-beat units. The connection between verse and body, Viereck claims, proves that our very bodies cry out for poetry, need it to feel whole, in step as it were.

It's easy to imagine swinging arms and tapping fingers to Shakespeare's sonnet:

> *Shall I compare thee to a summer's day?*
> *Thou art more lovely and more temperate:*
> *Rough winds do shake the darling buds of May,*
> *And summer's lease hath all too short a date.*

But—although this collection does include formal, metrical verse—there's no Shakespeare, nor any Edgar Allan Poe in it. All but one of the poems here were originally written in English—and all are recordings of the authors made after the advent of recording equipment. Here, we begin with the first great American modern poet, Walt Whitman, recorded more than a century ago, in 1890. He reads four

the same, how can you tell whether or not the poet agrees with the speaker? The answer, as usual: pay close attention. Sometimes you can tell and sometimes the best you can do is guess. But it's always worthwhile to look into the matter.

tone—the attitude of either the speaker or the poet. Usually, tone is attitude toward the subject matter of the poem. (Is the poet or speaker respectful? satirical? bored? hostile?) Much less often the word *tone* is used to mean attitude toward the audience.

voice—a word that can mean
  • the personality of the speaker or poet
  • the distinctive aspects of a poet's style
  • **persona**

Forms

ballad— Originally, ballads were folk poetry, written in short, musical, rhyming stanzas. Often they told sad, tragic, sometimes gory stories. People still write ballads all the time. Love poems, popular songs, and story poems often take the ballad form.

blank verse— unrhymed iambic pentameter. *Not* the same as **free verse**, which has no meter.

concrete poetry—
verse that takes the
shape of its subject.
confessional
poetry—a direct
and truthful kind of
verse, seemingly
about the facts of
the poet's life.
Confessional poetry
seems to tell us
secrets, shocking
material from which
we normally turn
away. This kind of
poetry has always
existed, but with
poets in the 1950s
and 1960s such as
Robert Lowell,
Sylvia Plath, and W.
D. Snodgrass,
confessional poetry
became a kind of
movement.
Confessional poetry
challenges us to
remember the
difference between
the poet and the
speaker, even when
we're seemingly
being told "this
really happened *to
me*."
couplet—a pair of
lines that seem to
belong together,
often because of
rhyme or stanza
form
dramatic
monologue (also
called soliloquy)—a
poem spoken by a
single speaker,
imagined as alone
and speaking to him-
or herself, exploring
his or her situation
or point of view
epigram—a very
pointed poem, often
very short. Here is
one from a friend of
mine:

lines from his 1888 poem "America!"

> *Centre of equal daughters, equal sons,*
> *All, all alike endear'd, grown, ungrown, young or old,*
> *Strong, ample, fair, enduring, capable, rich,*
> *Perennial with the Earth, with Freedom, Law and Love.*

Of all the readings in this collection, Whitman's is the only one that may not be genuine. There's lots of evidence to point to its authenticity, including correspondence from Thomas Edison indicating that he wanted to record Whitman (and Whitman—who was such a self-promoter that he reviewed his own book of poems—was clearly the type who would have liked to have been recorded), and the poem read is relatively obscure—an unlikely choice for a fake. But the original wax disc from which it supposedly came remains missing, casting doubt on this reading. Still, the very possibility of hearing Walt Whitman's voice is too good to pass up.

Many of us (especially those over 35) still carry fragments of poems heard in childhood in our heads. Often, these are occasional poems: Whitman's elegy to the assassinated President Lincoln:

> *O Captain! my Captain! our fearful trip is done . . .*

Or Henry Wadsworth Longfellow's:

> *Listen, my children, and you shall hear*
> *Of the midnight ride of Paul Revere.*

But sometime in the past 30 years or so, most students stopped memorizing and performing poems—and started studying them. By now, the people who read poems are mostly poets themselves or academics in a literature program. The majority of the rest of us grew to consider poetry as incomprehensible and inaccessible.

Ironically, a lot of people lay the accountability for this decline in the appreciation of poetry directly on the manuscripts of the man widely regarded as the greatest poet in English of the twentieth century, T. S. Eliot. Eliot's poetic experimentation, which came to be known as modernism, won him friends and foes. William Butler Yeats, the other, earlier giant of twentieth century poetry (both writers were awarded Nobel prizes), deplored Eliot's dark vision and rejection of the old poetic forms. (Alas, Eliot's estate would not allow the use of any of his many recordings for this collection, so only one of these titans is heard reading.)

Yeats' "The Lake Isle Of Innisfree" was written in 1892 (when he was 27 years old), and Yeats called it "my first lyric with anything in it of its own music." The poem begins with a biblical reference from the book of Luke:

> I will arise and go now, and go to Innisfree,
> And a small cabin build there, of clay and wattles made;
> Nine bean rows will I have there, a hive for the honey bee,
> And live alone in the bee-loud glade.

Compare this to the opening lines of Eliot's poem, published in 1915 but written as early as 1911 (when he was 23 years old), "The Love Song Of J. Alfred Prufrock." In it Eliot also reimagines the world in which he lives, but not as an idyll, rather as a grim place, made soulless by the industrial revolution:

> Let us go then, you and I,
> When the evening is spread out against the sky
> Like a patient etherised upon a table;
> Let us go, through certain half-deserted streets,
> The muttering retreats
> Of restless nights in one-night cheap hotels
> And sawdust restaurants with oyster-shells:
> Streets that follow like a tedious argument
> Of insidious intent
> To lead you to an overwhelming question . . .
> Oh, do not ask, "What is it?"
> Let us go and make our visit.

39

Here lies a woman,
Mrs., Miss, or Ms—
Now it doesn't matter
which it is.

Epigrams are not always funny, but good ones always *tell*.

epitaph—a kind of **epigram** memorializing a deceased person

free verse—poetry that avoids regular meter and rhyme schemes

ghazal—an adaptation of an Arabic verse form. A ghazal is a series of couplets; the couplets may rhyme, or they may simply repeat a phrase in the second line of each couplet.

haiku—a Japanese poetic form. In English, haiku are **syllabic**, usually arranged in three lines, with syllables numbering 5-7-5.

performance poetry—verse intended for public performance. Good performance poetry has all the virtues of good presentation— immediacy, emotional impact, power.

prose poem—a form that presents poetic language in unlined form

soliloquy—see **dramatic monologue**

sonnet—a poem in fourteen lines. Really, that's about it. Sonnets can be of almost any line length, rhymed or unrhymed.

stanza—a group of lines that appear to belong together. In traditional, rhymed poetry, each stanza takes the same form. In **free verse**, a stanza may be of any form or length.

syllabic poetry—verse written according to syllable count. In one kind of syllabic poem, each line contains the same number of syllables. In another kind of syllabic poetry, the poet cooks up stanzas in which the lines all have different fixed syllable counts: 1/5/9/13/9/7 and so on.

Traditions

allegory—a poem (or other artwork) that expresses universal human truths via fictional characters and actions, all of which have symbolic meanings

Anglo-Saxon—see **Old English**

canon—an authoritative list of the best or most significant poems (or paintings, songs, or other kinds of art). Canons can help us understand the history of poetry and can help us form our own ideas of what's good. But they have been abused. Don't let canons push you

Where Yeats' lyric makes brief reference to the Bible, Eliot's long poem is loaded with allusion—from Dante (in Latin) to Shakespeare to then-contemporary fashion statements.

Eliot's poetry is quite beautiful to the ear, but its scholarship proved an irresistible challenge to academics and critics who seemed more interested in understanding Eliot than in enjoying him. Thereafter, much of American poetry became something different, something denser and more difficult. And less fun.

There are many who think that the truly great poet of the twentieth century is William Carlos Williams, who also revolutionized the form. He reads his groundbreaking 1923 poem, "The Red Wheelbarrow":

> so much depends
> upon
>
> a red wheel
> barrow
>
> glazed with rain
> water
>
> beside the white
> chickens

There are those who think that, had more Americans encountered Williams' deliberately humble, amusing, and unpretentious verse in school, rather than that of Eliot, the state of poetry would be a whole lot healthier today.

As it is, sales of poetry books are low. When's the last time you saw someone reading a book of poems on an airplane? Even a literary novel might sell 25,000 copies; a book of poetry is tearing up the charts if it sells 1,500 copies.

A few twentieth century poets, notably Ogden Nash and John Ciardi, have made quite a good living selling poetry (although Ciardi did a lot of other types of writing as well), much of it a highly accomplished form of light verse. Others earned their money in different vocations: William Carlos Williams was a physician, Wallace Stevens an insurance company executive. But the vast majority of today's poets work in universities and support themselves by teaching others to write.

In the academy, a poet's income may be relatively secure, but—until recently—his or her audience was getting ever smaller and more obscure.

Now, something interesting and exciting is happening. Attendance at readings by literary poets is up all over the country. At the annual Conference on Southern Literature held in Chattanooga, Tennessee, hundreds of locals buy tickets, put on their best clothes, and go to readings by the great living Southern writers (fiction and poetry). In Kansas City, the Midwest Poets Series routinely draws a couple of hundred people who want to hear poets such as Galway Kinnell and Tess Gallagher. A glance at any Sunday's *New York Times* will turn up at least a half dozen poetry readings. In fact, it's to the point where poets spend almost as much time on the road as those itinerant bards of ancient Greece—and, like their ancient counterparts, they can pretty much count on making more money (considerably more) from readings and performances than from book sales.

And literary poetry is not the only verse on the rise. So-called popular poetry is experiencing a grand resurgence: Witness the boozy fun often found at a poetry slam, where a bar or coffeehouse audience plays a form of *The Gong Show* with dueling writers. Lately, there's also a devoted audience for the folksy warmth of cowboy poetry readings (Rhino has even released a CD, *The Cowboy Poetry Gathering*, recorded in Elko, Nevada). And everybody wants to be a rap star, where there's serious money to be made from a huge audience. Rap music, of course, is descended from the African-American poetic tradition of rhyming put-downs called "playing the dozens."

The reasons why people want to hear poetry read are varied. One is that we still fall in and out of love, watch sunsets, marry, and die—and what do we have to express that?

around. Like what you like.

comedy—a poem (or other artwork) that celebrates the persistence of humanity. Comedy has to do with people succeeding in some delightful way. Most comedy is funny, and most comedy ends well. One kind, **black comedy**, makes humor out of material we would ordinarily regard with dread.

convention—a general agreement about how to do something. Just as you find conventions in fashion (men's ties) or social behavior (handshakes), so you find poetic conventions. In **epic** poetry, for example, there is the convention of the **epic hero**'s descent into hell. In much love poetry, the loved one is described in conventional ways. A cliché (*cherry lips*—ugh—for example) is a convention that has died of overuse.

didactic poetry—verse that strongly advocates a point of view (e.g., **political poetry**) or aims to teach its audience (e.g., **moral poetry**)

dramatic poetry—verse that is meant (or is appropriate) for performance by actors

elegy—a poem of lamentation or sorrow

epic—a long public poem telling the story of how a community or nation came to be formed. A central figure called the **epic hero** faces the forces of nature, descends into hell, and risks life and limb in other **conventional** ways to bring the community into being.

genre—a type or kind of literature, poetry, or art: for example, **comic**, **epic**, or **tragic** poetry. Each genre brings into play a characteristic form or subject matter.

light verse—poetry that is playful or humorous. Light verse is usually rhymed. Sometimes people speak as if light verse were somehow "less important" than other kinds of poetry. Bunk.

lyric poetry—a catch-all term for short (usually), personal (usually), musical poetry. Lyric poetry normally is contrasted with **epic** poetry (which is communal in nature) and **dramatic** poetry (which is, well, dramatic). When most people think of poetry, they think of lyric poetry.

myth—a story that

Network television gives us toilet humor, cable brings streams of curses punctuated by violence, movies blow things up. But when we want to express ourselves as more fully human, as creatures capable of elevated thought and means of expression—then we have few places to turn. Poetry books may seem out of reach to some, but hearing a poem read is soothing and healing and helps to put us in touch with our true feelings.

And when we hear a poem read, we participate in an ancient tradition that ties us to our ancestors and to our community.

This box is meant to provide a sampling of some of the best poems in English of the twentieth century. It draws from the most prominent audio collections in the country: Caedmon, the Library of Congress, *New Letters On The Air* (a syndicated radio literature series of which I was producer and host for 13 years), Watershed, and many other private and public collections.

Certainly, the voices of the towering figures of poetry are in this box, but other poets are still relatively young: whether their work will be celebrated 100 years from now remains to be seen.

More important, and interesting, the twentieth century American poetry community in all its diversity of style and participation is represented. There are the modernists (Williams, Pound, etc.) and their successors the postmodernists (whatever that means); the free verse poets (just about everybody these days) and the believers in rhyme, the New Formalists (nobody wants to be called this); the Language poets (John Ashbery); the Beats (Allen Ginsberg, Jack Kerouac, and Anne Waldman); the feminists (May Sarton and Sylvia Plath); the lesbian feminists

Photo © Dorothy Alexander

Carolyn Forché

(Adrienne Rich and Audre Lorde); and the overtly political writers (Marge Piercy, Muriel Rukeyser).

There are funny poems to be found here (Ogden Nash, Lawrence Ferlinghetti, David Ray), and ironic ones (e. e. cummings, Charles Simic); sad poems (Carolyn Forché, Rita Dove, James Ragan) and lots of love poems (Richard Wilbur, Robert Penn Warren); poems with an edge (Charles Bukowski); lush poems (Richard Howard, Derek Walcott); poems read to music; poems written with and without rhyme or meter. Some of the poems are written by Christians (Donald Revell), some by Jews (Dan Jaffe), and others by Zen practitioners (Gary Snyder).

Charles Bukowski

But perhaps the most exciting development in this box, and in contemporary poetry as a whole, is the increasing participation of minority voices. Clearly, poetry is no longer the sole province of white men. Choosing a number of fairly young, minority poets for this box was a conscious decision and a reflection of what I find most exciting and engaging in literature today. Always, I have felt that my first obligation was to great writing and that great writing is best served by those with something fresh and challenging to say. More than any other writers, those of color have the ability to introduce us to new worlds, new ways of seeing the world, and exciting ways to use language.

African-American writers have long been important figures in American poetry, and one of those represented here, Langston Hughes, is an established poetry giant. (Alas, Gwendolyn Brooks would not give permission to include her work.) Rita Dove, a Pulitzer prize-winner and former Poet Laureate, writes about the massacre of blacks in the Dominican Republic by then-President Miguel Trujillo. Maya

examines or explains the universe, a culture, or persistent and profound human questions or truths. Some well-known examples are the myths of Icarus and Daedalus, Paul Bunyan, and Superman.

narrative poetry—verse that tells a story

occasional poetry—poems written for specific occasions, such as births, deaths, marriages, battles, and invitations to supper

Old English—the earliest recorded version of English, spoken from before the 500s to shortly after the 1000s. Also called **Anglo-Saxon**, this is the language of *Beowulf* and other fine poetry. Many of the short, concrete, gruff words in English—*stone, man, house, knife*—are from Old English.

After the French invaded England in 1066, English changed rapidly. Middle English was spoken between 1100 and about 1500, Early Modern English between 1500 and 1750, and after about 1750 or so, just plain Modern English.

parody—a poem (or other kind of art) that makes fun of another poem (or other kind of art)

periods—For convenience, we imagine history as being divided into periods, within which writers and artists are supposed to have something in common. Yes, this practice is a fiction of convenience. Chaucer would have been surprised to hear that he was *medieval*. We've created periods to help us understand history and how poetry fits in. Here are some of the major periods of English and world literature, along with the length of time they cover. (These are my wildly approximate guesses, because almost everybody disagrees.)

Homeric—1000 B.C. to about 750 B.C.

Classical—750 B.C. to A.D. 476

Dark Ages—476-1000

Medieval—1000-1450

Renaissance—1450-1660

Enlightenment—1660-1798

Romantic—1798-1832

Victorian—1832-1901

Edwardian—1901-1910

Modern—1910-1945

Postmodern—1945 - present

And there are subdivisions and

Angelou contributes her anthem for black women, and Al Young, Amiri Baraka, and Michael S. Harper all take inspiration from jazz.

Participation by Native Americans is a more recent advent on the poetry scene, despite the fact that probably no group of people has an older oral tradition. Here, you'll hear American Indian poets in a frank discussion of the clash between the ancient world and the one in which they live now: Joy Harjo on Anna Mae Pictou Aquash, an American Indian Movement member who was killed by the FBI (Harjo also plays the saxophone on this track); Adrian Louis on alcoholism among Indians; and Luci Tapahonso—who often writes about Navaho ritual—with a charming and hilarious poem about a young woman in a bad relationship with an Indian cowboy.

Four Latino writers read in this collection, among them Jimmy Santiago Baca, who learned to read and write while in prison, and Luis Rodriguez, who took up poetry after leaving a Los Angeles street gang. Carmen Tafolla has a Ph.D. but tells of her troubles with speaking English as a second language.

The youngest poet included is Indonesian-born Li-Young Lee. Lee's grandfather was the personal physician to Mao Tse-tung and his father a Christian revival preacher who was jailed in Jakarta and later moved to the United States. Lee's poem, "My Father, In Heaven, Is Reading Out Loud," sounds at times like the thoughts of any young man who feels himself a disappointment to his father, at other times, like the true experience of an exile:

> . . . but I don't disparage scholars;
> my father was one and I loved him,
> who packed his books once, and all of our belongings,
> then sat down to await instruction
> from his god, yes, but also from a radio.
> At the doorway, I watched, and I suddenly
> knew he was one like me, who got my learning
> under a lintel; he was one of the powerless,

to whom knowledge came
while he sat among
suitcases, boxes, old
newspapers, string.

The only poem not originally written in English in this box was also written by an exile. Joseph Brodsky came to America after serving time in prison in his native Russia. Here, he won the Nobel Prize and was named Poet Laureate (a job he loathed, calling it "ill-defined and underpaid"). I included Brodsky long before his recent death because the idea for this collection came out of a brainstorming session he and I had in a hotel room in Aspen, Colorado, during the summer of 1991. A year later, when I presented the idea to Richard Foos, the founding president of Rhino, he (much to my amazement) liked the idea and decided to act on it. Getting from there to here has been an enormous task, but one well worth the effort.

My hopes for this collection are many: Mostly, I want it to bring pleasure and to stir all sorts of emotions; then, I hope it will give a strong overview of what the last century of poetry has been like. Finally, it should prompt further interest in poetry and in language—an interest that will translate itself into reading and writing and reverence for the great gift of self-expression through words. And the better we are able to express our thoughts, ideas, fears, and emotions, the better we'll be able to communicate with—and perhaps even love— one another.

—*Rebekah Presson*
1996
dedicated to my husband Dewey F. Mosby

Joseph Brodsky

sub-subdivisions.

satire—a poem (or other kind of artwork) that holds up a particular social behavior for ridicule for the purpose of amendment

tragedy—a poem (or other artwork) that explores human limits by recounting the downfall of an admirable but flawed figure (the **tragic hero**). Tragedy explores how character is fate and vice versa.

verse—another word for *poetry*. Sometimes the word *verse* is used to distinguish metered, rhymed poetry from other kinds. The word *verse* may also mean
• a single **line** of poetry
• a single **stanza**
• **light verse**
Verse, is what it could be.

"Words You Might Hear Other People Use When They Talk About Poetry" excerpted from the book It Could Be Verse; Anybody's Guide To Poetry, by John Timpane. Available at your local bookstore. Or order from Ten Speed Press 1-800-841-2005.